Contents

CLASSIC FESTIVAL SOLOS offer the advancing instrumental soloist an array of materials graded from easy to more challenging. An assortment of musical styles has been included to give variety and to allow an opportunity for the musician to develop interpretive skills.

Jack Lamb, Editor

CHANSON RUSSE

Themes from **TSCHAIKOWSKY'S C MINOR SYMPHONY**
Arr. by **NORMAN GOLDBERG**

4

POLKA

FRANZ von SUPPE
arr. by NEAL PORTER

TRIO AND MENUET

G. F. Handel
Trans. by R. Christian Dishinger

EL 03729

7

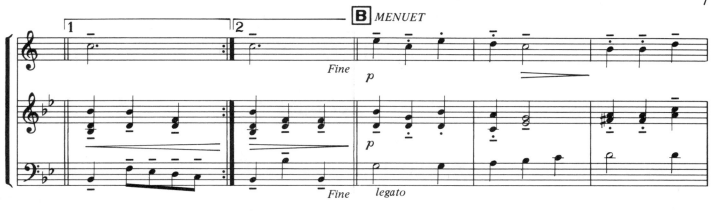

D.C. al Fine with all repeats

EL 03729

BUTTON WALTZ

ARTHUR NIX
Arr. by DAVID FERREIRA

*Gentle waltz tempo

*NOTE: Feel Free to use rubato. Not to be played in strict time.

EL 03729

9

IF I WERE THE KING

MOZART
Arr. by NORMAN GOLDBERG

KEMP'S JIG

Anonymous
transcribed by **R. Christian Dishinger**

EL 03729

EL 03729

LA CUMPARSITA

G. RODRIQUEZ
Arr. BELDON LEONARD
ASCAP

EL 03729

16

EL 03729

DREAM WORLD

BELDON LEONARD
ASCAP

Andante expressivo (♩ = 80)

19

EL 03729

HARBOR ECHOES

RALPH R. GUENTHER

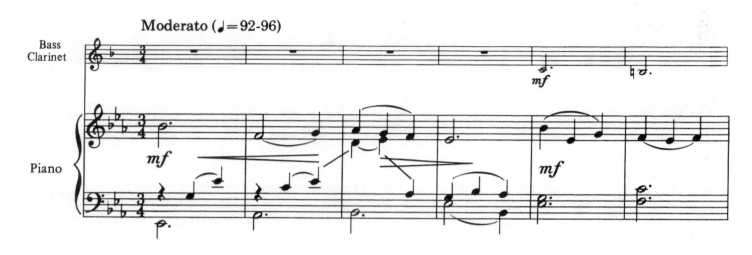

EL 03729

22

EL 03729

WALKIN' HOME

ARTHUR NIX
Arr. by DAVID FERREIRA

*NOTE: Soloist should <u>not</u> syncopate the 3rd beats at letters B and F.

EL 03729

ROYAL MARCH

J.S. BACH
Arranged by Ralph R. Guenther

EL 03729

28

Performance Time = 1' 40"

GAVOTTE

J.S. BACH
Arranged by Ralph R. Guenther

Tempo di Gavotte (♩=56)

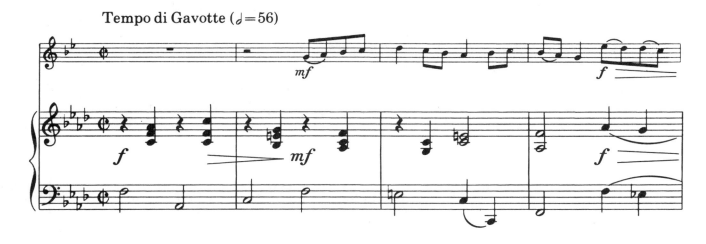

EL 03729

NORWEGIAN DANCE

EDVARD GRIEG
Arr. by NEAL PORTER

Quietly and gracefully

EL 03729

TWO GUITARS

This characteristic Russian melody is traditionally written in two-four meter, yet is also traditionally played with a definite feeling of four beats to the measure. The metronome marking ♩ = 50, could also be indicated ♪ = 100.

In the opening theme, each note of the solo part should be played as staccato (short) as possible so as to imitate the plucking of the guitar strings.

Arr. Beldon Leonard

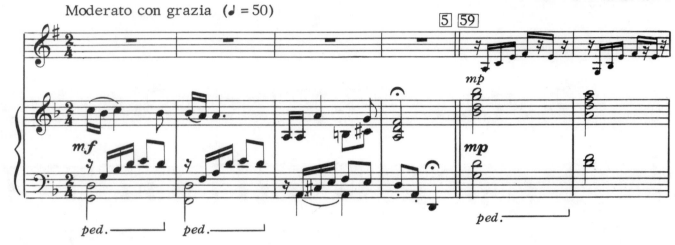

EL 03729

36